# AT HOME IN THE BIOME

# CORAL REEF

Louise and Richard Spilsbury

WAYLAND

First published in Great Britain in 2016 by Wayland

Copyright © Wayland, 2016

Editor: Sarah Eason
Cover design: Lisa Peacock

Produced for Wayland by Calcium
All rights reserved.
Dewey Number: 577.7'89-dc23
ISBN: 978 0 7502 9755 4
10 9 8 7 6 5 4 3 2 1

Wayland
An imprint of
Hachette Children's Group
Part of Hodder & Stoughton
Carmelite House
50 Victoria Embankment
London EC4Y 0DZ

An Hachette UK Company
www.hachette.co.uk

www.hachettechildrens.co.uk

# Contents

# At Home in the Reef

Coral reefs are one of the world's most colourful **biomes**. These amazing, rock-like structures grow on the ocean floor near coastlines around the world. Coral reefs can be as small as a coin or as large as an entire island. Many are home to thousands of fish and other animals.

## Colourful Colonies

Coral reefs are formed from living animals, called **polyps**, that live in large **colonies**. These animals build hard skeletons to support and protect themselves. Over time, the skeletons join together and form a coral reef. Coral reefs develop in warm, shallow waters, where there is plenty of sunlight. They provide shelter from strong waves, and many plants and animals grow on them. Animals come to coral reefs to feed and have their young, too.

Sponges are very slow-moving, plant-like animals that attach themselves to coral reefs. These tube-like creatures take in **nutrients** and **oxygen** from water that passes through them. They are an important part of the biome. They are homes for reef animals and plants, and help to keep the reef alive by joining corals together.

Sponges on a reef are covered with tiny holes. These take in water that is later pumped out from the top of the sponge tube.

5

# Corals

Coral polyps are very small, so a coral reef can be made up of hundreds of thousands of these creatures. Why do these strange animals create huge, rock-like structures called reefs and how do they feed?

## A Coral Skeleton

Corals build their hard skeletons out of **calcium carbonate**, the same substance that shellfish take in from the water and use to make their shells. Coral polyps create layers of calcium carbonate beneath their bodies, forming a skeleton. They live on top of the skeleton. Over time, new polyps live on the skeletons of dead ones, making the skeletons larger. That is how a reef grows bigger.

There are thousands of different types of corals. They spread their **tentacles** to catch food to eat.

**HOME SWEET HOME**

Corals use their stinging tentacles to catch and eat tiny living things that float in the water. Corals also contain plant-like **algae** that use sunlight to produce their food through **photosynthesis**. Corals provide the algae with shelter, and the corals feed on some of the nutrients that the algae produce.

# Sea Stars

Sea stars, also known as starfish, are star-shaped animals that use their long, pointed arms to crawl over a reef in search of food. Many sea stars have five arms, but some have 10 or 20 arms. A few have as many as 40 arms!

## On the Attack

Most sea stars eat **molluscs**, such as clams. A sea star climbs onto the shell of its **prey**, and uses its arms to pull on the shell. When the shell starts to open, the sea star shoots its stomach out through the mouth on the underside of its body. It pushes the stomach inside its prey's shell to feed. If a sea star loses an arm when it attacks, it can grow another. Some sea stars shed damaged arms or lose them to escape from **predators**.

Scientists have started to call these star-shaped creatures sea stars rather than starfish because they are not fish at all! They are more closely related to sea urchins, which also have a spiny covering to protect them from predators.

HOME SWEET HOME

Sea stars move slowly around a reef using hundreds of little tube-like feet on the underside of their arms. These little tubes take turns to suck on a surface and then let go. This action helps sea stars to move.

# Sea Slugs

There are many different sea slugs and they come in a lot of incredibly beautiful colours. Many are small, but some of these soft-bodied molluscs can grow as large as 30 centimetres long.

## Slug Stalks

Some sea slugs feed on algae that grow on coral reefs, and some live on animals such as sponges or plant-like, meat-eating sea anemones. A sea slug finds food using the two large, horn-like tentacles on its head. These parts can detect tastes and scents in the water, and can be drawn back under the slug's skin to protect it from predators.

Unlike most other molluscs, sea slugs do not have a shell for protection. Some have dull colours that blend in with their surroundings so predators do not see them. Some are brightly coloured and contain foul-tasting poisons, so when fish eat the sea slugs, they quickly spit them out, unharmed. Their bright colours warn predators that they taste bad, so they learn to leave the slugs alone.

A sea slug moves on a flat, broad muscle on the underside of its body called a foot. Some sea slugs can swim short distances in the water by rippling their muscles.

# Clownfish

Clownfish are named for their bright, stripy colours and the way they dance and dart around. These fish are **adapted** to living among the poisonous sea anemones that grow on coral reefs. The anemones keep clownfish safe from predators that dare not get too close to the anemones' deadly tentacles.

## A Shelter That Stings

Before a clownfish can live among an anemone, it swims around, brushing parts of its body against the anemone's stinging tentacles. This seems to help a clownfish become **immune** to the fish-eating anemone's sting. A clownfish never strays more than 30 centimetres from the anemone that it lives in.

A clownfish eats leftover fish that the anemone catches. The clownfish keeps the anemone healthy by eating its damaged tentacles and tiny animals that could harm it. The clownfish's droppings also provide nutrients.

**HOME SWEET HOME**

The black stripes between the orange and white colours are different widths on different types of clownfish. Clownfish that swim among the tentacles of larger sea anemones have thick, dark black stripes. This helps to **camouflage** the clownfish among the shadows of the anemone's moving tentacles.

# Butterflyfish

There are more than 100 types of butterflyfish. Most of them have brightly coloured bodies and pretty markings like those found on butterflies. Butterflyfish are one of the most common fish on coral reefs around the world.

## A Clever Snout

The butterflyfish spends its days searching among the coral for food. The unusual long, thin shape of its mouth can fit into small gaps in the coral that other fish cannot reach. This pointed snout allows the butterflyfish to pull out coral polyps, worms and other small animals to eat.

**HOME SWEET HOME**

Butterflyfish feed during the day and rest in the coral reef during the night. At night, butterflyfish swim into dark openings in the reef. Their bright colours and markings fade so that they blend into the background. This keeps them hidden from dangerous predators such as snappers, eels and sharks.

*To keep them safe while they are feeding, many butterflyfish confuse predators with the round, eye-like patterns on their backs. Predators do not know which end of the fish to attack and in which direction the fish might try to swim. This gives the butterflyfish a chance to escape.*

15

# Seahorses

Seahorses are a very special type of fish. They have a head that looks like a horse and a long, snake-like tail that can grip things.

## Sucking Up Supper

Seahorses swim upright, but they cannot swim very well so they use their tails to grasp onto corals. This stops waves from washing them away. They sit still and wait for small plants and animals, such as shrimp, to float by. Then they suck up their food through their snouts, like a vacuum cleaner. To keep safe while they feed, seahorses are covered in hard, bony **plates** that stop many predators from eating them.

Seahorses have good eyesight to help them spot prey and to keep a lookout for any predators on the reef.

## HOME SWEET HOME

Seahorses can change colour very quickly to match their surroundings. Many have incredible forms of camouflage that help them hide from predators, such as crabs and other fish, around the reef. Some seahorses are not only the same colour as the coral they feed on, but they also grow bumps and lumps that make them look exactly the same as the coral!

17

# Octopuses

Octopuses can see well, even at night, which is when they hunt on coral reefs for food. During the day, octopuses can squeeze their soft, flexible bodies into spaces in the reefs, where they can safely rest.

## On the Move

The undersides of an octopus's eight long arms are covered in suckers. The octopus uses these suckers to pull itself along a reef. It also uses them to grip, feel and taste things. When the suckers find food, the octopus bites into its prey using its hard, pointed beak. If an octopus's arm is damaged, another arm grows in its place. An octopus can also swim up to 40 kilometres per hour by squirting water backwards. It sucks water into its body and shoots it out again.

## HOME SWEET HOME

Many octopuses can change colour quickly to look like the coral they are resting or feeding on. This camouflage keeps them safe from moray eels, sharks and other predators.

The main part of the octopus's body, called the mantle, looks like a big bag. An octopus draws water into the mantle and through its **gills**, and then shoots the water out of the mantle to move itself forwards.

19

# Pufferfish

Pufferfish have an amazing tactic for surviving life on a coral reef. When a predator comes near, this ordinary-looking fish suddenly puffs itself up until it is several times its normal size. This makes it very hard for a predator to fit a pufferfish in its mouth!

## All Puffed Up

Pufferfish have stretchy stomachs, so that when they swallow large amounts of water, they can quickly inflate themselves. Most pufferfish have spines on their skin that stick out only when they are puffed up, which makes them look even less tasty to enemies. Many pufferfish also contain a poison to put off attackers. It tastes bad and is strong enough to kill other fish. Some pufferfish have colourful markings to warn animals that they are poisonous. Others blend in with their background.

A pufferfish delivers its poison through spines on its back. If a predator bites into a pufferfish while it is grazing on the reef, the attacker gets a nasty and possibly deadly surprise.

HOME SWEET HOME

A pufferfish has four big teeth that are joined together to form a hard beak. Using strong jaw muscles, it can open and close its beak to crack open crabs, clams and other molluscs. It also uses its beak to scrape the algae that it eats off the reef.

# Moray Eels

Moray eels are long, brightly coloured, snake-like fish that can grow up to 4 metres long. Unlike other fish, a moray eel does not have fins on the sides of its body. Instead, it swims around the coral reef by moving its body from side to side, and it can even swim backwards.

## A Moray's Mouth

At night, a moray eel feeds on fish, molluscs, squid and crabs that live on coral reefs. It uses its excellent sense of smell to find prey. When it senses a victim is nearby, it uses its large teeth to grab the prey and tear into it. The moray eel also has a second set of teeth that can shoot forwards and drag prey into its throat.

*Moray eels are covered in slime that protects them as they move through the rough, rocky spaces in a reef.*

## HOME SWEET HOME

Moray eels are fearsome predators, but they are hunted by larger sea animals such as sharks and barracudas. That is why they wriggle into cracks and holes among the coral reef during the day. They stay in these hiding places to keep them out of sight from predators, and so they can attack passing prey animals, too.

# Giant Clams

Giant clams that live on shallow coral reefs are the heaviest molluscs in the world. An adult giant clam can grow to nearly 1.2 metres long. Once the clam has settled in one position on a coral reef, it stays there for the rest of its life.

## Open and Shut

Giant clams are made up of two hard, zigzag-shaped shells that are attached with a hinge so they can open and close slowly. The colourful part you can see just inside the opening is the soft mantle. The mantle has two openings, called siphons. Giant clams use one of the siphons to take in water. They take in oxygen from the water to breathe, and tiny pieces of food to eat. Then they spit the water out of the other siphon, which looks like a tube.

Like corals, giant clams have billions of algae living inside them. The algae use sunlight to make food by photosynthesis. In return for a safe place to grow, the algae provide food for the giant clams.

The mantle of a giant clam can be yellow, red, green, blue, pink, or brown, or a mixture of colours. No two giant clams have mantles of the same colour.

# Reef Sharks

Whitetip reef sharks are long, slim sharks that have short, blunt snouts. They are named for the bright white tips of two of their fins, and because they are often seen swimming over coral reefs in search of food.

## Terrible Teeth

Whitetip reef sharks rest in spaces in the coral during daytime and come out at night to feed. They swim over the reef alone or in small groups, stopping to poke their snouts into each crack and hole in the reef they find. They mostly find fish, octopuses and other prey using their senses of smell and hearing. When they find prey, reef sharks grasp it and pull it out with their small, sharp, pointed teeth.

# HOME SWEET HOME

A reef shark is long and thin. Its top fin is positioned lower on its back than on other sharks. This allows the shark to twist and push its body deep into a hole in the coral to reach prey. In fact, some reef sharks even use their bodies to block holes so the prey cannot escape!

Whitetip reef sharks have large, round eyes that help them search for prey in dim light and at night.

# Reefs Under Threat

Coral reefs have been forming for about 500 million years, but today they are under threat. Reefs are damaged by **pollution**, such as rubbish and chemicals. Divers harm reefs, as do the anchors of fishing ships or their nets, which drag across the reefs. Reef fish are caught for people to eat or to keep in aquariums. One of the biggest threats to reefs is **climate change**. As temperatures rise, corals turn white and die.

## Protecting Our Coral Reefs

Many people are trying to protect and restore coral reef biomes. In some places, people build **artificial** reefs for reef animals to live on. Some reefs, such as the Great Barrier Reef in Australia, are protected by law. **Conservation** groups also raise money to protect **endangered** coral reef animals, such as staghorn corals.

People are working to protect and restore staghorn corals like these, and to save important coral reef biomes.

**HOME SWEET HOME**

Staghorn corals get almost all the nutrients they need from the algae that live within them. The corals also get their colour from these algae. As ocean temperatures rise, the algae die. The corals lose their colour and look bleached, or white. They no longer have enough food, and may die.

# Glossary

**adapted** Changed to survive in an environment.

**algae** Plant-like living things that do not have leaves but make food using sunlight.

**artificial** Made by people rather than occurring naturally.

**biomes** Communities of plants and animals living together in a certain kind of climate.

**calcium carbonate** A white substance found in animal shells.

**camouflage** A colour or pattern that matches the surrounding environment and helps an organism to hide.

**climate change** The increase in Earth's temperature thought to be caused by human actions such as burning oil, gas and coal.

**colonies** Groups of animals living together in one place.

**conservation** The act of guarding, protecting or preserving something.

**endangered** When a plant or animal is in danger of dying out.

**gills** Body parts that fish and some other animals use to breathe underwater.

**immune** Protected against something.

**molluscs** Animals with a soft body and often a hard outer shell, such as clams and snails.

**nutrients** Chemicals that living things need to live and grow.

**oxygen** A colourless gas in the air we breathe.

**photosynthesis** The process plants use to make their own food.

**plates** Hard, armour-like discs.

**pollution** When something is put into water, air or land that damages it or makes it harmful to living things.

**polyps** Small animals that produce hard skeletons that can join together to form coral reefs.

**predators** Animals that catch and eat other animals.

**prey** An animal that is caught and eaten by other animals.

**tentacles** Long, flexible animal arms.

# Further Reading

Anita Ganeri, *Exploring Coral Reefs: A Benjamin Blog and His Inquisitive Dog Investigation* (Exploring Habitats with Benjamin Blog and His Inquisitive Dog), Heinemann-Raintree, 2014

Camilla de la Bedoyere, *Coral Reefs* (100 Facts), Miles Kelly Publishing, 2010

Jinny Johnson, *Watery Worlds*, Franklin Watts, 2015

Niki Foreman, *Shark Reef* (DK Readers), Dorling Kindersley, 2014

Seymour Simon, *Coral Reefs*, HarperCollins, 2013

# Websites

Find out more about coral reefs on the BBC's website at:
**www.bbc.co.uk/nature/places/Great_Barrier_Reef**

For stunning pictures, facts and more visit:
**www.kidsdiscover.com/spotlight/coral-reefs**

Discover how important coral reef biomes are:
**http://wwf.panda.org/about_our_earth/blue_planet/coasts/coral_reefs**

# Index